KNIGHT-CAPRON
LYNCHBURG
LYNCHBURG, VA
WITHDR

WRITERS OF THE DAY

GENERAL EDITOR: BERTRAM CHRISTIAN

H. G. WELLS

KNIGHT-CAPRON LIBRARY
LYNCHBURG COLLEGE
LYNCHBURG, VIRGINIA 24501

By IVOR BROWN

NOVELS:

YEARS OF PLENTY
SECURITY
LIGHTING-UP-TIME

POLITICS:

THE MEANING OF DEMOCRACY
ENGLISH POLITICAL THEORY

Camera-Portrait *Hoppe*
H. G. WELLS

H. G. WELLS

By
IVOR BROWN

FOLCROFT LIBRARY EDITIONS / 1972

PR
5776
.B7
1972

Library of Congress Cataloging in Publication Data

Brown, Ivor John Carnegie, 1891-
  H. G. Wells.

  Reprint of the 1923 ed., issued in series:
Writers of the day.
  Bibliography: p.
  1. Wells, Herbert George, 1866-1946.
PR5776.B7 1972   823'.9'12   72-8641
ISBN 0-8414-0396-1 (lib. bdg.)

H. G. WELLS

By
IVOR BROWN

London
NISBET & CO. LTD.
22 BERNERS STREET, W.

First published in 1923

Printed in Great Britain
by The Riverside Press Limited
Edinburgh

"HIS was a naturally irritable mind, which gave him point and passion, and moreover he had a certain obstinate originality and a generous disposition. So that he was always lively, sometimes spacious, and never vile. He loved to write and talk. He talked about everything, he had ideas about everything; he could no more help having ideas about everything than a dog can resist smelling at your heels. He sniffed at the heels of reality. Lots of people found him interesting and stimulating, a few found him seriously exasperating. He had ideas in the utmost profusion about races and empires and social order and political institutions and gardens and automobiles and the future of India and China and æsthetics and America and the education of mankind in general."

Description of Mr Britling in
Mr Britling See It Through

CONTENTS

		PAGE
I.	Shops, Schools and Suburbs	9
II.	Journalism; Science; Fiction	21
III.	Art Kipps and Some Others	37
IV.	The Social Scene	47
V.	The Human Limitation	62
VI.	Faith and Mr Britling	79
VII.	The Hope that is in History	99
VIII.	Since the War	112
	Bibliography	120
	American Bibliography	123
	Index	126

I

SHOPS, SCHOOLS AND SUBURBS

LITERARY explanations are fashionable and sometimes amusing, but they are rarely useful. The great subject of the explainers has been Shakespeare, and some of them have explained him clean out of any literary existence whatsoever. To these people it seems inconceivable that a country lad could kindle a light of poetry that has blazed unquenchably across the world. Others have explained Shakespeare otherwise; recently a distinguished French critic discovered how it was that a mere Stratford boy could have the gift of imagining. It was because he was born within a hundred miles of the Welsh border. He must have been part Celt! This judgment is more complimentary to the Celt than commendatory of the critic. Genius bloweth where it listeth. Charles Dickens

H. G. WELLS

came out of a blacking factory and J. M. W. Turner out of a barber's shop. The people who try to explain away Shakespeare into the essence of a literary ghost, because no Warwickshire bumpkin could have built such powerful rhyme, ought certainly to engage themselves at once in explaining H. G. Wells. How could the draper's boy of 1880 have held in 1920 the listening continents in fee ? At the time of the Armistice Woodrow Wilson had the ear of the world to an extent unknown by any living man before. He failed and passed. That sovereignty over the minds of men was transferred in no small measure to H. G. Wells, who found himself, at the time of the Washington Conference, with an audience measured by tens of millions. That was partly due to the system of " syndicating " newspaper articles, so that millions of readers of various nations could read the same articles at about the same time. But the fact of syndication does not explain the choice of him whose views were to be given this gigantic range and sway. To explain

SHOPS, SCHOOLS AND SUBURBS

why Wells is listened to is the object of this book; to explain why Wells is a genius —why, in short, he emerged from an unsuccessful suburban shop in London and journeyed by way of servants' hall and drapers' counter to his present sovereignty among the minds of men, a position alike magnificent and merited—is beyond any man's power. Perhaps our Frenchman will discover an explanatory Celtic strain. But there is no need for sensible people to do more than admit that destiny plays its game in secret and does not limit the divine fire to feeding upon such fuel as wealth and opportunity provide.

Herbert George Wells was born at Bromley, in the Kentish section of Greater London, on September 21st, 1866. His father combined shopkeeping with professional cricket; his mother was the daughter of a Sussex innkeeper and had been a lady's maid. Joseph Wells, the father, who was the son of the head gardener at Penshurst Castle, Kent, made a failure of his little general store; but he did some redoubtable things at cricket, things worthy of the great Kentish cricketing tradition. In *Wisden's Almanac* the name of Wells, J., will be found in the Cricket Records, at the head of the list of those who have taken, in first-class matches, four wickets in four successive balls, a kind of super hat-trick. He did this at the expense of Sussex batsmen in 1862 ; it had not been done before, or no record had been kept if it had. And after Joseph Wells came in that list better-known names : Ulyett, Lockwood, Mold, Brearley and Trott—the cream of cricketing company.

Owing to the failure of the shop Wells' mother went back to a superior sort of " service." She became housekeeper at Up Park, near Petersfield, and the boy here experienced the solemnities of decaying feudalism (see the Bladesover section in *Tono-Bungay*) before he was sent out into the world to shift for himself. He was marked down for the paternal occupation of selling things and at the age of thirteen he was behind a chemist's counter. Later he was tried

SHOPS, SCHOOLS AND SUBURBS

" in the drapery " at Southsea. Fortunately he was a failure. His employers, I suppose, found him restless, subversive, "too clever by half." At any rate the boy looked over the counter to a vague thing that was stirring outside, " higher education." He jumped the counter and grasped this thing, working his way up by grants and scholarships to the Normal School of Science at South Kensington, in the great and growing University of London. There followed study under Huxley and a degree with first-class honours in zoology. Also, in his own words, there was "scampering about London to attend great political meetings, to hear William Morris on 'Socialism,' Auberon Herbert on 'Individualism,' Gladstone on 'Home Rule,' or Bradlaugh on 'Atheism.'" It was a parsimonious and persistent struggle for learning and opportunity that suggests the students of the Scottish tradition. After this came a period of schoolmastering in St John's Wood; there was a mishap in the playing fields and a long illness, during which Wells took to writing for the papers

H. G. WELLS

to pay his way. Then writing took hold of Wells. "Some little kink in my mind," as he has himself put it, "has always made the writing of prose very interesting to me." He began with short articles, criticisms and so on, received the encouragement of W. E. Henley and then, harnessing science to creative fancy, began his series of scientific romances. The first of these, *The Time Machine*, was published in 1895 (the author was then twenty-nine). It is called "an invention," and it deserved that proud title to the full.

I began this chapter by deprecating literary explanations of the ancestral and ethnographical kind. But, if heredity is of little help in the interpretation of Wells and his work, environment is of incalculable importance. Wells was born on the edge of a London that was still Dickensian, a city not a county; but in his boyhood and in his student days he saw this monster of streets and stucco rise and stretch itself and sprawl in shabby chaos over the countryside. He saw the submersion of villages and of the old

SHOPS, SCHOOLS AND SUBURBS

village semi-feudal conventions. He saw everywhere development unplanned and undisciplined. He saw the decline and fall of Victorian England, not as Arnold Bennett was seeing it from among the furnaces and pit-heads and pot-banks of North Staffordshire, not as John Galsworthy was seeing it from Harrow and Oxford and the Forsyte windows round Hyde Park, but from the squalid disorder of the new suburbs. Wells is one of the first citizens of Greater London; he felt its growing pains and cursed the absent physicians who let the young giant shoot all ungainly out of its clothes and prescribed no regimen to give it health proportionate to its size. Let him speak for himself. The wonderful picture of Bromstead in *The New Machiavelli* supplies the perfect reaction to the boy's environment of that young monster, Greater London.

"That age which bore me was indeed a world full of restricted and undisciplined people, overtaken by power, by possessions and great new freedoms, and unable to make any civilised use of them whatever ; stricken now by this idea and by that, tempted first by one possession and then another to ill-considered attempts ; it was my father's exploitation of his villa gardens on the wholesale level. The whole of Bromstead as I remember it, and as I saw it last, —it is a year ago now—is a dull useless boiling-up of human activities, an immense clustering of futilities. It is as unfinished as ever ; the builders' roads still run out and end in mid-field in their old fashion ; the various enterprises jumble in the same hopeless contradiction, if anything intensified. Pretentious villas jostle slums and public-house and tin tabernacle glower at one another across the cat-haunted lot that intervenes. Roper's meadows are now quite possibly a slum ; back doors and sculleries gape towards the railway, their yards are hung with tattered washing unashamed ; and there seem to be more boards by the railway every time I pass, advertising pills and pickles, tonics and condiments, and such like solicitudes of a people with no natural health or appetite left in them. . . . Well, we have to do better. Failure is not failure nor waste wasted if it sweeps away illusion and lights the road to a plan."

To a plan! There, in three syllables, is the heart of the Wellsian creed. All his work is an amplification of that excellent saying of another: "It was the function of the nineteenth century to liberate; it will be the function of the twentieth to control." Here is Bromstead in liberation and "this freedom" is no more than this futility, this anarchy, this squalor of jerry-building and money-grubbing and sham gentility. What was becoming of youth in this new world of gigantic expansions? The youth of the upper middle class was spilling over the brim of the old public schools into the new nineteenth-century foundations—the Marlboroughs and Haileyburys and Cliftons and Cheltenhams. For the rest, for the millions, there were the National Schools, where young Mr Polly was crammed mechanically by an undertrained and underpaid staff with various subjects that his mind could not possibly entertain. This to be followed, if the child were fortunate, "by a private school of dingy aspect and still dingier pretensions, where there were no object lessons and the studies of bookkeeping and French were pursued (but never effectually overtaken) under the guidance of an elderly gentleman, who wore a nondescript gown and took snuff, wrote copper-plate, explained nothing, and used a cane with remarkable dexterity and gusto!"

Well, Squeers had gone and feudal Bladesover was turned to a more modern Bleak House, and there were movement, change, ebb and flow of men and money and, sometimes even, of ideas. At any rate it was a fluid world, not so fluid as the Forsytes dreaded, but fluid enough for a Denry Machin to rise from Staffordshire humility to pomp and power and circumstance in London. Bennett reacts with a detached and often humorous realism to this continuous crumbling of the aristocratic and rise of the commercial order, Galsworthy with irony and pity. Wells is never detached. He does not so much pity as protest.

SHOPS, SCHOOLS AND SUBURBS

He bangs with a will upon his secular pulpit, preaching on the deadly perils of a Bromstead world. He is always seeing the moral of the muddle; sometimes his moral adorns a tale, sometimes it is given a purely pamphleteering expression. Always he is seeing the ethics of the business, crying out for light, order, discipline; not always consistently in detail, for, like Walt Whitman, he might have said: "Do I contradict myself? Very well then, I contradict myself. I am large. I contain multitudes." But in essence his philosophy is one, as it is a philosophy of the One. The *Outline of Bromstead* is the fraction of which *The Outline of History* is the whole.

The jostle and jumble of Greater London is but the microcosm of which the anarchy of nations is the macrocosm. And the remedy is not beyond us, not undiscoverable if only there be "love and fine thinking." There is always a creative side to Wells' satire. Bromstead does not drive him, like Timon, to the woods, there to cry out upon the world and spit defiance at destiny. It drives him

H. G. WELLS

no farther than to his study. But it drives him as reformer, not as recluse. It drives him to *First and Last Things*, to *The Research Magnificent*, to *The Salvaging of Civilisation*. It drives him, through history and science, " to a plan."

II

JOURNALISM ; SCIENCE ; FICTION

WELLS' first book was published in 1895, when the author was in his twenty-ninth year. There was nothing of the young prodigy about him as a writer ; he had been too busy earning a living and recovering from the oppression of that necessity to publish masterpieces in his teens. And there is nothing remarkable about Wells' first book. It is a collection of a dozen articles published in *The Pall Mall Gazette* with two additional sketches. It is entitled *Select Conversations with an Uncle*.

It is not remarkable, one may repeat, but it is fresh, readable and swift in motion. Neither perhaps fresher nor more readable than other young journalists might have turned out, but good enough. The imaginary uncle, a wealthy South African, is a nice blend of the man of the world and the man of ideas. His "Theory of the Perpetual Discomfort of Humanity" is excellent, the idea being that reforms always come so tardily that they overtake an entirely new set of reformers, who find the old, belated reforms very little to their taste. The essay shows Wells as a beginner, and a shrewd beginner, in the craft of prophecy. "Ireland, when Home Rule comes home to it, will fairly howl with indignation." That is not bad for 1895. And in the vigorous avuncular philosophy we get a foretaste of the vigorous Wellsian prose, with its hearty statement of dislikes.

"Your average humanity I figure as a comfortable person like myself, always trying to sit down and put its legs somewhere out of the way, and being continually stirred up by women in felt hats and short skirts, and haggard men with those beastly, long, insufficient beards and soulful eyes, and trumpet-headed creatures, and bogles with spectacles and bald heads."

Again of such people he says: "They go about flapping their ideals at you." There

JOURNALISM; SCIENCE; FICTION

germinates Wells, the hot critic of ineffectiveness. Was it this gift of invective that caught the eye of W. E. Henley and John Lane?

This first volume of Wells is worth a glance. It is worth looking also at the publisher's advertisements at the end. What was the literary world into which Wells was advancing, sedately enough, but so soon to break into a gallop and to lead? It was the world of *The Yellow Book*, the queer muddled world of the nineties, in which a book-lover could choose between the latest anger of John Davidson and the latest diablerie of Beardsley. How extraordinary now seems the list of contributors to *The Yellow Book*! In volume four, for instance, Richard Garnett and Victoria Cross go side by side. It was a time without a "school" —not that Wells would have fitted into any school. The Wessex Novels were coming to a close. Shaw was emerging. Kipling, who matured far younger than most people remember, was at the height of his swift-gathered power. Henley was in flood. Æstheticism ebbed.

H. G. WELLS

Wells went into this world, but he was not of it. He was too big for any literary compartment. Jingoism, even in its idealised form of Imperialism, did not attract. The pettifogging pessimisms and æstheticisms of little poets and essayists passed him by. He needed no inspiration from outside, for he throve on his own plethora of ideas as the young Redwood and the Cossars throve on the Food of the Gods. In literary stature he grew apace; in literary output he kept the printers busy and the reviewers in search of new phrases. He started late and he arrived early. *The Time Machine* appeared in the same year as *The Select Conversations*. Again, it was reprinted work. A note on the fore-page says: " The substance of the first chapter of the story and of several paragraphs from the context appeared in *The National Observer* in 1894. *The Time Traveller's Story* appeared almost as it stands here in the pages of *The New Review*." The book is dedicated to W. E. Henley. In the same year came also a volume of tales, *The Stolen Bacillus and*

JOURNALISM; SCIENCE; FICTION

Other Stories, and a fantasy, *The Wonderful Visit.* It was more than a gallop : it was a charge.

Within the limits of space imposed on this small book it is obviously impossible to deal with the early work in detail or in close analysis; the rich quantity and quality of his later writing puts that out of question. A dated bibliography will be found at the end of this volume, in which the so-called "scientific romances," along with the other books, are recorded in their chronological order. I do not propose therefore to do more than summarise the main features of mind and method in these first stories, amplifying this with some particular allusions.

If Wells was on the gallop, so too was science. Science, we may say, was the charger on which he rode, and it was moving very fast then, as now. Moreover the public was becoming increasingly interested in science, and here was the man who brought to science a unique gift for popular expression and a penetrating vision for its future possibilities. The early books are usually called "scientific romances," but we have to be careful about that word "romance." Wells was not treating science in any wild spirit of hey-go-mad. As later discoveries and theories have shown, he was simply dealing in plausible futures, some less plausible than others. But he was not, as the word is popularly understood, "romancing." He was simply showing what might happen to man if he exploited the new knowledge that had come to him in sudden spate as Aladdin exploited his lamp. Relate *The Time Machine* to Einstein; relate all the tales of coming war to the war that did come and, more tragic still, to the kind of fatal fury of scientific destruction that any future war may release. Wells, regarded from this standpoint, is certainly not "a romancer." He is an imaginative realist.

It was natural that a pupil of Huxley's should have his mind upon the enthralling subject of evolution. *The Time Machine* is a good story, with some superb descriptive passages of the waning of the world, and

JOURNALISM; SCIENCE; FICTION

carried along by a remarkable gift of narration; it is also a study of evolution's possibilities. The Time Traveller, whose curious machine snatches him into the future almost to the extent of a million years, finds that humanity has been cleft into two sections: the Eloi and the Morlocks. The Eloi are the successors of the masters, the Morlocks of the labourers. The Eloi " had decayed to a mere beautiful futility." Science had made the world too easy for them. They lived delicately on the servile Morlocks, who had been degraded to the level of subterranean serfs, gross mechanicals, mere fractions of men, but who were yet capable of blundering revolt and blind fury. " The Nemesis of the delicate ones was creeping on apace." Super-man had put himself in the grip of sub-man, because his seeming security had put a premium on feebleness. Disease had been stamped out and social triumphs effected. And the result was atrophy of mind and muscle, the declension from the sovereignty of the world to a pitiful and perilous decay.

H. G. WELLS

Here then, in the first of the scientific stories, Wells emerges as masterly narrator and acute sociologist. Fascinated by the conception of power through knowledge he visualised power so vast and so well applied that it would abolish any need for power, or indeed for effort of any kind. But there is more in it than that. There is the conception of the utter futility of power unless it is applied with wisdom to the harmonising of human relations. Power in this case has created a slave-state. Scientific power in the hands of the unscrupulous vivisectionist (*The Island of Dr Moreau*) might create artificial humans by the surgical treatmentof animals.

"Then I took a gorilla [said the doctor] and upon that, working with infinite care and mastering difficulty after difficulty, I made my first man. All the week, night and day, I moulded him. With him it was chiefly the brain that needed moulding: much had to be added, much changed. . . . I taught him the rudiments of English, gave him ideas of counting, even made the thing read the alphabet."

JOURNALISM; SCIENCE; FICTION

Mingle these two ideas of power misapplied—the idea of the emasculated Eloi and brutalised Morlocks and the idea of Dr Moreau's artificial man—and all the elements of "Rossum's Universal Robots" are at hand. Dr Capek, the Czecho-Slovakian dramatist who in 1922 astonished the world with his play on the Robots (*R.U.R.*), was only giving effective dramatic form to conceptions that arose nearly thirty years before in the maturing brain of the young English scientist-author.

Power outrunning man's ability to control power, science blindly playing at Frankenstein, that is the basic philosophy of much in the early novels. Man so busy at mastering nature that he overlooks the necessity for putting human relationships in proper order was a natural notion for one who contrasted the ordered energy and application of the laboratory with the disorderly squalor of the acquisitive, competitive world outside. In *When the Sleeper Wakes* (1899. Afterwards published in a revised and altered edition as *The Sleeper Awakes*) there

H. G. WELLS

is a vision of the world as it might be two centuries hence. Again the picture is of a progress purely mechanical, of a scientific servile state. The roads move by machinery, human nature stands still. Here are some reflections of the man who has awoken from a trance of two hundred years' duration.

"He tried to figure the individual life. It astonished him to realise how little the common man had changed in spite of the visible change in his conditions. Life and property, indeed, were secure from violence all over the world, zymotic diseases, bacterial diseases of all sorts had practically vanished, everyone had a sufficiency of food and clothing, was warmed in the city ways and sheltered from the weather. . . . But the crowd was a crowd still, individually cowardly, individually swayed by appetite, collectively incalculable. . . . He thought of the hopes of his vanished contemporaries, and for a moment the dream of London in Morris's quaint old *News from Nowhere* and the perfect land of Hudson's beautiful *Crystal Age* appeared before him in an atmosphere of infinite loss."

JOURNALISM; SCIENCE; FICTION

The story ends in a riot of class-war, the people rising against the gigantic financial international trust in whose bondage they had been held. The apparent peace of the world had been a peace of Cæsar, a mere deadness concealing disharmonies so violent that the peace could not be durable. Organism moves out against the tyranny of mechanism, and the still, small voice of human rights overbears the roaring of the great machines. In a preface to the later edition of this book Wells is modest about its virtues. As a story it has limitations, but it is compact of the early Wellsian philosophy and essential to an understanding of his views.

There is another current to Wells' reflections on power. Suppose there should be no internationalism, no peace of Cæsar? What then? Power still grows, science marches. Their end, then, will be just human destruction, nothing better. Instead of the class-war there will be the war of the nations, in which man, being lord of his machines but not of his own passions, will hurl himself to

H. G. WELLS

ruin in a whirlwind of crashing aeroplanes amid a fury of eternally detonating bombs. On this thesis was written *The War in the Air* (1908) and *The World Set Free* (1914).

As an early forerunner of this series there is *The War of the Worlds*, in which the idea of a Martian invasion is developed. The Martians are creatures with hypertrophied intellect, unhuman and therefore unmerciful. They are, in this war, a breed of super-Robots, man having raised himself above good and evil into an arid paradise of power. Again Wells is more than the student of science without human values: he is the eager protestant against it.

So far stress has been laid on the sociological aspect of Wells' early fiction. To do so is essential, but it is also unfair unless an equal stress is laid upon its worth as good story-telling. There is practically nothing written by Wells which lacks gusto. He seems to go literally running to his desk with delight and, though he must often have been as weary of his pen as a great cricketer may be of his bat, his greatness comes out, as

JOURNALISM; SCIENCE; FICTION

does the cricketer's, because of the unfailing delight in invention and technique and the doing of the job. Mr J. D. Beresford has classed some of these early books as "the novels of exuberance," an admirable definition. Wells' finest expression of exuberance is in *Mr Polly*, which I shall consider later. But exuberance comes brimming over even in the scientific stories. Some of them, particularly the earliest, are not to be related to any philosophy in particular. The author just releases his keen, receptive mind among the teeming possibilities of the laboratory. What might happen should men defeat gravitation? They might visit the moon. Conceive the reactions of a stolen bacillus on the fate of man, conceive the future of man should a food be discovered that produced regular instead of intermittent growth. Giants would arise in the land, thriving on this "Food of the Gods," and the Wellsian fancy and humour thrive fast enough on giants. Conceive an invisible man, or conceive again, in purer fantasy, the arrival on our shores of mermaid or angel. What will

H. G. WELLS

these creatures make of us or we of them ? A little philosophy creeps into the answers, but the joy of the answer is mainly in sheer narrative skill. Wells, answering these questions, is at his lightest and liveliest. The free play of his darting, inquisitive mind moves him as sack moved Falstaff, that sack which " ascends me into the brain ; dries me there all the foolish and dull and crudy vapours which environ it ; makes it apprehensive, quick, forgetive, full of nimble, fiery, and delectable shapes ; which, delivered o'er to the voice, the tongue, which is the birth, becomes excellent wit." The percipient creator of visible, risible Bert Smallways must not be forgotten, as we admire the imaginative creator of atomic bombs, time machines and invisible men.

Bert Smallways is the little Cockney caught up in *The War in the Air,* an innocent infant of the Frankenstein family. The great ones let loose monstrosity, the little ones are eaten up. This is tragedy, the tragedy of war. But at the back of every tragedy there is comedy, as behind every comedy there is

JOURNALISM; SCIENCE; FICTION

tragedy. It all depends upon the mental selections of the looker-on. Wells, looking on, has as sharp an eye for the humour as for the horrors of progress. The reactions of a world-war upon Bert are the work of a great artist in humour, particularly in the most essential humour which is shot with wistfulness and pathos. It was not a mere whim that made Wells take Charlie Chaplin to his Essex home. The two men have a comic sense, a comic genius in common. The tragi-comedy of the little man at odds with a great and baffling universe, always a trifle befogged in his wits and yet stronger at heart than all the forces of mechanism, is a theme dear to both of them. Wells brought to the so-called "scientific romances" a tenderness in humour that he has not always maintained, and as a born master of character he could always adorn his picture of a merciless mechanical progress with a rare bloom of human comedy. One leaves this first phase of Wells with the mental vision of a runaway horse called Science, striding in a mad gallop of

H. G. WELLS

destruction none knows whither. And on his back, half delighted, half terrified, wholly unable to control this unmanageable mount, is some poor petty human, preferably a Londoner, slang on his lips and courage in his heart, riding the monster as he might ride a roundabout on Hampstead Heath. A tragic rider to the sea, if you will, and yet, as the nursemaids say, "What a little jockey!"—one who will jest as he takes his final toss. . . . But we are anticipating Mr Kipps.

III

ART KIPPS AND SOME OTHERS

IN the first chapter of this book Wells was described as ranging through history and science " to a plan." But Wells would never have won his gigantic public had he been a sociologist only. A telescoped proverb has been made out of two Latin tags—" Dulce et decorum est desipere in loco." Wells is a master of the light dalliance of literature as he is of its intellectual austerities. He has as keen an eye for the fun as for the muddle of the market-place. He can bask in the mellow sunshine of human frailty as he can rise to the moral and political challenge that blows up like a tingling wind from that same fallibility. He will build you a new world in the twinkling of an eye; but his own eye can twinkle as he surveys the hearts and hopes of men. The dividing line between

H. G. WELLS

tragedy and comedy is a shadow indeed. Both deal in futilities, frustration, the gap between ambition and achievement. The jealous husband has been the centre of a thousand farces: he is also Othello. It all depends on the artist's point of view. The world remains, the emphasis differs. So with Art Kipps. His translation to " Society " affords the contortions of a fish out of water, and contortions have their humorous side; but the fish gasping out its little life has as much tragedy for the artist as the dying gladiator. So is there a tragedy of Kipps as there is a tragedy of Charlie Chaplin amid the wild antics of *The Kid*. Mr Polly deserves to live amid the grand clowns of English letters. Yet Polly is as plaintive as a puppy, lost, hungry, and woebegone in a crowded London street.

Wells discovered his vein of human comedy early. First came *The Wheels of Chance* (1896), then *Love and Mr Lewisham* (1900). *Kipps* followed in 1905, and *Mr Polly* in 1910. There was a throw-back to this novel as a war-time relaxation in

ART KIPPS AND SOME OTHERS

Bealby (1915). Mr Lewisham stands a little outside this group, more sad-eyed and pensive. He hovers on the verge of the ridiculous, instead of splashing gaily into it. He is a figure for compassion, and his romance of grey streets has a wistful beauty about it that I find nowhere else in the vivid, arresting and sometimes ruthless artistry of Wells. Hoopdriver, the central character in *The Wheels of Chance*, is a shop assistant. So, too, are Kipps and Polly. Lewisham is an usher and a penniless student of science at South Kensington. Wells has gone back to his youth for his comedy, but there is nothing of the drab diarist in his method. The author is fairly revelling in his sense of the world he knows, not just passing it on to us at second-hand, but giving it back, as all true artists do, at a higher power, quickened and enlarged by the unique reactions and sensibilities of an ardent, pitying personality. I think that the pity is important. I have heard it said of Wells that he is insensitive, and too widely, too easily derisive. But in the stories of the under-dog there is compassion of a high and delicate quality.

You may, of course, find " propaganda " in these books, but you will certainly do wrong if you set yourself to find it. Nearly all fiction has implicit appraisals and condemnations of the world; the mind must judge as surely as the ears and eyes record. Once again, as in the relation of comedy to tragedy, it is a matter of emphasis. Often Wells emphasises political and economic judgment as the business of fiction with the hammering impact that will not be denied. But in the group of novels with which this chapter is concerned the emphasis is on the play of personality. Indirectly you gather that schoolmastering is drudgery on a pittance, and that the kind of snobbish little centres of misinformation where Lewisham teaches and Kipps learns are not vessels of light but plague-spots on the body politic. That Cavendish Academy, with its " loads of catechism " and infamous travesty of mental training, burns in the reader's mind. Indirectly, too, you gather that shop-

ART KIPPS AND SOME OTHERS

assistants live meanly, sweated, bullied, fobbed off with scraps of cheap and nasty recreation in the great years of youth. They who should be opening their minds and bodies to the light are devouring bread and scrape in subterranean dining-rooms that reek of oilcloth and cold mutton fat, and feeding their immortal souls, at great cost to their mortal eyes, on the vile prints turned out by the great factories of trash to meet the minds of the quarter-educated and the purses of the quarter-starved.

That and much more of social instruction you may get from the romances of Lewisham, the escapades of Hoopdriver on holiday, the poignant exaltation of Art Kipps, the boisterous chivalry of Mr Polly. But you will get instruction by side-winds as mere whisperings of the atmosphere, and not by the straight hurricane of social pamphleteering that carries the later novels on their course. In all these stories the story counts, and the characters are greater than the creed. We may lay the books down as better citizens, but that fact is only what Beetle would have called a "giddy parergon." The real point is that while we are holding the books up we are engrossed in the human comedy, pricked to a keener relish of the invincible spirit of man, and given reason to rejoice that not all the shabbily pretentious academies nor all the serf-infested emporia have broken down man's power to kick his heels in the prison-house, and to carry into some hideous street of Clapham or into the frowsty parlour of a small gents' outfitter the unquenchable ecstasy of romantic escapade. The reader of Art Kipps' fortunes may, if he will, dig out the raw material for a first-rate Fabian tract. But he would be better advised to let such betterment be and concentrate, if I may be pardoned the pun, on Art for Art's sake.

I have already alluded to Wells as the novelist of the new, anarchic, Greater London. He rarely gets outside the Home Counties, and more and more the Home Counties are ceding their rural individuality to the Cockney's march. Kipps and Mr Polly are not Londoners, but they are

ART KIPPS AND SOME OTHERS

Cockneys. They have the Cockney's superb self-mastery, his power to rise to an occasion. Kipps could be meek enough in the shop, but see him when he is out walking with Helen Walsingham and they are charged by a random bull. " He directed her to walk quietly towards the stile, and made an oblique advance towards the bull. ' You be orf,' he said " ! I submit that " You be orf " is as perfect as it is precise. It breathes the very spirit of that London pride which can never see any reason why foreign bodies, human or animal, should not be regarded as a joke or, at most, a very trivial terror. Bert Smallways in *The War in the Air* is another of these admirable self-sufficients.

It is because Wells has such an eye for the Englishman of the south-east that he has carried on in these few books of his the tradition of Dickensian fun. Philosophically, Wells and Dickens are poles asunder. Dickens was not interested in plans or discipline, and his creed of liberty with kindliness, of fancy-free against social science, has found its modern champion in G. K.

H. G. WELLS

Chesterton. Wells once described Chesterton and Belloc in the following words:—"They present a conception of vinous, loudly-singing, earthy, toiling, custom-ruled, wholesome, and insanitary men; they are pagan in the sense that their hearts are with the villagers and not with the townsman, Christian in the spirit of the parish priest." Dickens would have loved these men, but there is certainly no room for them in some of the Wellsian Utopias. There they would be taught to wash and stiffen themselves and study the possibilities of drainage. This vision of a Catholic and Alcoholic Church has not appealed to Wells the sociologist.

But to Wells the novelist pure and simple such humours of the flesh are sheer delight. He depicts you a shady character with the true Dickensian gusto. Chitterlow, the down-at-heels playwright in *Kipps*, and Chaffery, the fraudulent spiritualist in Mr Lewisham's adventures, take rank with the great scamps of Dickens, with the Montague Tiggs and Chevy Slimes. There is gusto, too, in the lingering over flesh-pots. Dickens

ART KIPPS AND SOME OTHERS

could describe a meal as well as he could describe anything. Consider that wonderful Christmas banquet in the Gargerys' house on the marshes—" a leg of pickled pork and greens and a pair of roast stuffed fowls." Then mincepies, then plum pudding, and then—oh, stupendous tribute to the digestive capacity of the Gargerys and Mr Wopsle and Uncle Pumblechook—pork-pie to drive all home. Then consider the " funer-ereal baked meats " in *Mr Polly*, match Uncle Penstemon with Uncle Pumblechook, set the avuncular Kipps alongside of Mr Wopsle, and you find the same alert and joyous plunging in the waters of human oddity, the same gambolling revelry in the descriptive possibilities of crumbling mortality. Moreover the same vivacity is there, the same delight in the sheer rush of narrative, the same invention in the apt phrase for a human gargoyle, the same relish for any monster or manikin whose soul drops fatness. And certainly Mr Polly's spirit lards the pages through which it walks, trots and finally gallops in glory. As Mr Jingle cut everything to a word, so by contrast did Mr Polly put his lips to words as a boy puts his lips to a penny balloon and blew them out into a rare, preposterous magniloquence. " Sesquippledam verboojuice "—did ever tongue twist a phrase with a more inspired ignorance ? A distinguished critic has called *Mr Polly* the author's masterpiece. For my part I would keep such praise for *Tono-Bungay* and *Mr Britling*, but in all the lighter novels there is a sympathy as well as a boisterous sense of comedy that lifts them clear of farce into the keen air of true artistic vision.

IV

THE SOCIAL SCENE

WELLS was already climbing the heights of literary power as the nineteenth century died. The Eminent Victorians had passed. No sooner had these grave heroes gone than the intellectual world forgot its admiration and began to smile or even sneer at the heavy moral pressure of their work. The sage kernel of the Utilitarian creed had been thrown aside, along with its valueless shell. Imperialism was rampant, Liberalism at a low ebb. The Socialist pioneers of the eighties had said their say and oblivion was overtaking them. There was a common sense of disillusion. The terrific self-confidence of that great era of expansion had collapsed like an overblown flower. All through the century there had been a stalwart faith in democracy. It was believed that if you only set free man's mind and put a ballot paper before him he would know his own good and pursue it. The nineteenth century had believed in the rationality of man; it had forgotten impulse, inertia, herd morality. It had trumpeted " freedom broadening down from precedent to precedent." But the new generation held democracy to be a failure and Tennyson to be a rather sickly joke. In a few years a great and progressive sociologist, Professor Graham Wallas, shattered finally the democratic optimism of the old school with an epitome of realistic pessimism called " Human Nature in Politics."

Into this social scene stepped Wells, armed with an extraordinarily perceptive, imaginative and rapid mind, and a profound passion for sociological speculation. The environment which had in boyhood moulded his creed and temper had been the decaying feudalism of the Home Counties and the squalid, anarchic proliferation of urban life in Greater London. Immediately two ideas attracted him. One was the urgency of

THE SOCIAL SCENE

control. The other was the conception of the future as our possession, our challenge and our duty. The aimless "development" of the nineteenth century had been as purposeless as the path of a rudderless ship in uncharted seas. That development, that immense liberation of mechanical power and social forces, had to be taken in hand by rational men who knew what they wanted and how to reach a definite goal. The future of mankind had been treated either as a quasi-religious mystery or a preposterous jest. Wells thought otherwise, and still thinks otherwise. If our forefathers lived blindly for the day that is no reason why we should not live with purpose for the morrow. Their neglect of posterity is our call to thought and action. There could be a science of the future. If it were called Socialism and denounced in angry, petty prejudice, then minds must be disillusioned—by clear thought and keen argument. The tub-thumpers in the cause of reaction, the noisy conservators of muddle, called Socialism "the Beginning of the End." To Wells

H. G. WELLS

Socialism was the End of the Beginning, the dawn of purpose and control after a night of cloudy, lazy self-confidence, the clearing up of undisciplined growth, the salvaging from ugliness and futility of such spots as Bromstead, the co-ordination of orderly, political effort, the establishment of a plan.

In a sequence of three books—*Anticipations* (1901), *Mankind in the Making* (1903) and *A Modern Utopia* (1905)—Wells stated his constructive social criticism. Such work is, confessedly and inevitably, rough-edged. If there is a science of the future it is certainly not an exact science, but the more one dips back into these books the more one is struck by the certitude of much of their prophecy, the durable, detailed value of their counsel. That brilliant critic, Dixon Scott, wrote of Wells:

"Watch him roughing out a new house, a new State, a new Time, it is like seeing a master-draughtsman working with swift coloured chalks—dashing in towers with a touch, swirling out vistas, dropping details in their wake like gems. . . . It is the

THE SOCIAL SCENE

flashes and splashes and sudden, unforeseen sallies that are reliable, that reveal; it is the deliberate calculations that go wrong."

That is illuminating criticism when applied, as Dixon Scott applied it, to the later novels. But the point about *Anticipations* is that the deliberate calculations are so often right. Let anyone turn to that excellent essay in this volume on "The Life-History of Democracy." It foretells with quite uncanny exactitude how the modern democracies, "these governments of confusion," will drift to war through "jealousies and anti-foreign enactments, tariff manipulations and commercial embitterment." It also foretells the nature of that war. "The New Democracy will blunder into wars and the opening stage of the next great war will be the catastrophic breakdown of the formal armies, shame and disasters, and a disorder of conflict between more or less equally matched masses of stupefied, scared and infuriated people." We need not be too contemptuous surely of Wells' "deliberate calculations."

H. G. WELLS

The purpose of these books is to expound the idea of a " New Republic." The word " Republic " was not used vaguely for state or community; the republican as opposed to the royalist ideal is strongly stated, and there is angry criticism of " the crawling of body and mind " engendered in the stuffy atmosphere of a Court. The political theory which Wells advances is utilitarian in the sense that all public conduct and management must be valued by some practical test and not by some vague phrases like " The Rights of Man " or " Human Equality." Here is the Wellsian test as expressed in the first chapter of *Mankind in the Making* :

" Any collective human enterprise, institution, movement, party or state is to be judged as a whole and completely, as it conduces more or less to wholesome and hopeful births, and according to the qualitative and quantitative advance due to its influence made by each generation of citizens born under its influence towards a higher and ampler standard of life."

THE SOCIAL SCENE

Perhaps that is a trifle vague. But it demonstrates the type of utility which was to be the first criterion of the social scene. And there is nothing at all vague about the subsequent plans for setting the New Republic in being and for training in mind and body the New Republicans.

Those plans are far too detailed for discussion in an essay of this limited scope. One can only single out certain large points as instances. There is the matter of democracy, for instance, that large and loose idea upon which the nineteenth century had fastened with an almost unqualified delight. Wells could take as short a line with democrats in those days as Lenin or Mussolini later on. " I know of no case for the elective Democratic government of modern states that cannot be knocked to pieces in five minutes " (*Anticipations*, p. 123). " It is manifest," he explains, " that upon countless important public issues there is no collective will, and nothing in the mind of the average man except blank indifference." He goes on to discuss the limitations of " the grey voting mass." His mind, at that time, ran towards an aristocracy of character and intellect and in *A Modern Utopia* there is an analysis and classification of society on lines somewhat similar to those followed by Plato in his *Republic*, and suggestions are made for an order of " Samurai," voluntary nobility, like the body of Guardians in Plato. The Samurai are to be ascetic, but not necessarily austere, men and women devoted to the community, chosen by their gifts and developed by this training, to lead and teach and administer. They are to be knights-errant against muddle and waste and ignorance, the chivalry of statesmanship. The order of the Samurai, in fact, is the expression of a high and rather inhuman ideal. It is representative of one phase of Wells, the Wells that does not suffer fools gladly and is impatient with normality, short-tempered in controversy, and moved by an intellectual pride that only the greatness of the intellect in question could justify. The Samurai are not to every man's taste and one may be forgiven for guessing that if Mr Chesterton

THE SOCIAL SCENE

were asked what he thought of the Samurai he would express a preference for Sam Weller.

I do not think that Wells would now hold fast to the notion of these super-specialists in the guidance of their fellow-men. Since the war his attitude to democracy has been less intolerant, and his faith is in a general education for social life and social duty rather than in the segregation of a shining few. Probably, too, his adventures in the Fabian Society turned his thought and taste against oligarchy. During the years 1907 and 1908 Wells worked hard for Fabian Socialism and rendered the society good service. His *New Worlds for Old* (1908) is a fine statement of Collectivism that must have made many converts to Socialism, and his two Fabian tracts, *The Misery of Boots* and *Socialism and Marriage*, are important. But he could not agree with the Fabian " old gang " and withdrew his brilliant powers of pamphleteering to snipe at them rather than for them. A sharp criticism of Fabianism is made in Wells' contribution to a volume of essays called *The Great State* (1911). This criticism is made from a democratic standpoint and quotes Mr Belloc approvingly :

" It remained for Mr Belloc to point the moral of the whole development with a phrase, to note that Fabianism no longer aimed at the socialisation of the whole community, but only at the socialisation of the poor. The first really complete project for a new social order to replace the Normal Social Life was before the world, and this project was the compulsory regeneration of the workers and the complete state control of labour under a new plutocracy. Our present chaos was to be organised into a Servile State."

Fabianism he further calls " the first experiment in planning and one almost inevitably shallow and presumptuous." The Wells of this period is still Socialist in broad intention and ideal, but he disclaims the word because it has become so " battered and coloured and bent by irrelevant associations." His new ideal demands great

THE SOCIAL SCENE

individual freedom and the point against aristocracy is quite definitely stated.

"Nothing can be clearer than that the necessary machinery of government must be elaborately organised to prevent the development of a managing caste, in permanent conspiracy, tacit or expressed, against the common man. . . . Officialism is a species of incompetence."

And so on. We are plainly, in this anti-Fabian outburst, getting a long way from the ideal of the Samurai.

Wells, in fact, as his social theory developed, was realising what Plato never did realise: the inalienable humanity of humankind. Plato's Guardians were not men and women: they were embodied wisdom; functions, not personalities. So too his soldiers and workers were not conceived as individuals with passions and exaltations and agonies of their own, but simply as fragments of society, bits and pieces in the temple of progress. That kind of outlook on society is as fatal as the crassest individualism. The charge that the Samurai are functions and not people is less true than the similar charge against Plato's Guardians. But it has some weight, a weight which Wells soon acknowledged. One must remember that inside his brain there is always the artist's relish for humanity as well as the sociologist's relish for order. One cannot simultaneously love Mr Polly and the Samurai any more than one can conscientiously serve God and Mammon. The Dickensian strain in the Wellsian comedy makes for democracy even when cold reason bears hardly on " the grey voting mass."

As Wells lost sympathy with the furtive benevolence of Fabianism he did not abandon the word Socialism as representative of his political and economic aspirations. In *First and Last Things* (1908), a volume described as " A Confession of Faith and Rule of Life," he stands by Socialism, but with this condition:

" If I disavow the Socialism of condescension, so also do I disavow the Socialism of revolt. . . . If Socialism is only a conflict

THE SOCIAL SCENE

with poverty, Socialism is nothing. But I hold that Socialism is and must be a battle against human stupidity and egotism and disorder, a battle fought through all the forests and jungles of the soul of man."

A Socialist, immersed in the drudgery of agitation, propaganda and political or municipal politics, might turn angrily on the Wells of *First and Last Things* and cry out upon sentences like this: "As Christians have dreamt of the New Jerusalem, so does Socialism, growing ever more temperate, patient, forgiving and resolute, set its face to the World City of Mankind." "That," the critic might say, "is just gas. It's no use meeting the slum landlord, the sweating employer, the militarist bully with such pious gentilities. It's a fight, and no amount of your tranquil theorising will obliterate the fact."

To such an argument, natural as it is and in some ways cogent, one can only answer that there is a diversity of gifts and that such diversity is best acknowledged and respected. Wells is too big to be wasted on the soap-box or in the committee-room. He is, as sociologist, the embodiment of the leaping mind. His brain works so fast that it cannot always stop to consolidate the positions it has captured. Thus his Socialism is a series of intellectual thrusts, always brilliant, not always co-ordinated. He is not ashamed to recant or to abandon one hurriedly conquered position for another, seen suddenly and as suddenly seized. That is the paradox of all the Wellsian social theory. He is the preacher of Plan, but his plans are fluid and changeable. Disorder he denounces, yet to a lover of system his mind must seem disorderly. The Fabians pack their platterful of social wisdom in a neat, trim vessel. Wells is no hand at packing; his wisdom would be too much for any vessel. You must take him as you find him, abundant, various, inventive, clapping to your brain a kind of electrical high-frequency. And, so doing, you must take your choice from the flood of suggestion. The point is that the flood is real and unquenchable.

THE SOCIAL SCENE

Bernard Shaw's mind, with all its colossal argumentative power and the superb engine of its dialectical prose-style, is far stiffer than the mind of Wells. Shaw moulds sagacity hard and tight. Wells scatters it as a man throws gravel on a path. The reader must sort out the reason from the rhetoric, the mere glittering from the authentic gold. He can do so in full confidence that the reason and the gold are there.

V

THE HUMAN LIMITATION

BY the close of the first decade of the twentieth century Wells was more than an accepted man of letters in London and a keenly followed explorer in the avenues of social theory. His reputation had begun to march across the world and his presence in the drawing-rooms of the influential was a valued trophy for any of the Leo Hunter family who was cunning enough to snare him. One might even say, bold enough, for the lion had claws, and to be a hunter of Wells might result in a somewhat scarifying and crushingly veracious portrait in the next novel. None the less there were plenty of people willing or eager to risk that fate, just as there are plenty of rich people eager to pay heavily for the pleasure of submitting their need of portraiture to the merciless easel of an Orpen or a John.

THE HUMAN LIMITATION

Wells then had become an intimate of the people who run the country. So far he had been a critic and theorist of the ideas of government; now he became a critic and a theorist about governing people. He wrote less of the future and more of the present, less of Utopia and more of Westminster and Mayfair. As a small boy he had seen Bladesover from the servants' hall, and as a youth he had seen the ruling class of the Empire through the halfpenny paper and the windows of cheap lodgings—but now face to face. Hitherto Lady Sunderbund had smiled upon him from the pages of a society journal; now she lisped her fatuities in his ear.

His reaction to this experience was a new type of book, new for him, and new also for the world in so far as he blended the essay with the novel and philosophy with fiction, employing a fresh and, on the whole, successful literary method. *Ann Veronica* (1909) is a love story sharp-edged with controversial spines and thorns. *Tono-Bungay* (1909) is a magnificent social panorama, whose foreground is the supersession of a moribund feudalism by an active, vulgar, vastly adventurous commercialism. *The New Machiavelli* (1910) is a ferocious commentary on the governing class and a vivid study in sexual psychology. *Marriage* (1912) covers some similar ground, analysing the violent disharmony between " getting on " and finding peace of mind and spirit. *The Passionate Friends* (1913) is a return to the mood of *The New Machiavelli,* and is about as pallid as the work of so intensely keen a writer can ever be. *The Wife of Sir Isaac Harman* (1914) carries on the speculation about the position of educated women in the society of the time, no longer the pets of men, but not yet their equals in legality and status. *The Research Magnificent* (1915) combines the pursuit of political ideas with a sketchy fictional form even more markedly than in previous novels. The war overshadowed it, and with the war we reach a new and distinct phase of Wells' work, which must be left for later discussion.

These books, beginning with *Ann Veronica* and ending with *The Research Magnificent,*

THE HUMAN LIMITATION

have had their later counterparts, but since so enormous a convulsion as the war was bound to give a new orientation to Wells' thought they may be conveniently discussed as a group by themselves, the Big Pre-War Novels. I do not propose to analyse them in detail, but rather to look for common characteristics and a common significance.

In the first place these books are intensely personal and subjective in method. The view of London and its big-wigs which they present is the view consequent upon the immediate emotional and intellectual reaction of a man both intensely impressionable and intensely quick-witted. They were written while the mind was hot and they have all the virtues as well as the vices of that literary method. There is no detachment or subjection of the author's individuality to the pursuit of objective vision. "Emotion recollected in tranquillity" has no place here. Furthermore the emotion that is thrown straight on to paper is very often anger, sometimes scorn, but not, I think, malice. It may be suggested that the

H. G. WELLS

famous portrait of the Baileys in *The New Machiavelli* is an impression of Wells' Fabian days set down in malice. As a matter of fact that portrait, if carefully read without the will to malice on the part of the reader, is not so cruel as is generally supposed, and contains much genuine appreciation. Malice is a festering, lingering thing, and Wells' mind is altogether too quick for it. But anger there certainly is, and at times there is almost despair. *The New Machiavelli* is the darkest in tone of the series, and it is permissible to see Wells about 1909 and 1910 going through a black period, as Shakespeare went through a black period in the first years of the seventeenth century. On the other hand it is not in Wells to be a pessimist. His wrath is particular, not general. It is aimed against individuals, not the universe. Wells could never talk about destiny sporting with mankind, or complain that as flies to wanton boys are we to the gods. Even if we accept Britten's outburst in *The New Machiavelli* as the authentic view of Wells (a process for which

THE HUMAN LIMITATION

we have no real justification whatever) that does not constitute essential pessimism: "But of all the damned things that ever were damned, your damned shirking, temperate, sham-efficient, self-satisfied, respectable, make-believe, Fabian-spirited Young Liberal is the utterly damnedest." That, you may say, is no more than the eloquence of an undergraduate flown with insolence and audit ale. Whatever it is, it is an attack upon men, not upon man. It is an indictment of the present, not a statement about the future. True pessimism is something far more profound than a passing fit of disenchantment or a gusty outbreak of quasi-intellectual tantrums. It is a philosophic conviction that reason is not in the universe. Wells has never said that. He has, on the other hand, most strongly asserted the opposite. No man who has written as he has about the future or about religion can be ticketed as a pessimist—a label, by the way, of which I can see no reason to be ashamed, though it is commonly regarded as a black mark.

It is time to turn for a moment from this question of pessimism in order to explain the meaning of the phrase "The Human Limitation" which I have set at the head of this chapter. Wells had begun his literary work with an extraordinary vision of the possibilities of power, particularly of scientific power. Man's knowledge of the universe and his ability to bend and harness the forces and treasures of creation to his need and pleasure are not increasing like a heap of sand, grain by grain; they are developing with the ever-growing momentum of a body falling through space. If a hundred years of mental change have so altered the face of the earth and the range and scope of human power, what may we not expect from a thousand years of similar and probably intensified development of knowledge? Surely all the imaginable glories of all the imaginable kingdoms are in the grasp of man's hand, that now seems so petty, so faltering, so absurd. Even now there are accumulations of knowledge—and accumulations of wealth and opportunity where-

THE HUMAN LIMITATION

with to exploit that knowledge—which could alter in the briefest span of years our present sorry scheme of things. But who own the wealth and opportunity that hold that precious knowledge in fee? The privileged, possessing class. And what are they doing? They are at worst mere amateurs of horse and hound, at best mere fiddlers with the squalid intrigue of party politics. The modern world abounds in spacious opportunity, and is worked by the starveling will to use that opportunity. The future's horn of plenty seems to offer unlimited blessings, were it not for lack of character, courage and vision, in short " the human limitation."

But the trouble goes deeper than that. It is not merely that the place of power is dominated by the pomp and puerility of power or that the sphere of opportunity is cluttered up by functionless property-owners with giant purses and midget brains, and the tastes of barbaric children at large in a bear-garden of primitive delights. It is not merely that democracy has become " a grey confusion " in which spiritual pestilence abounds. There is the specific limitation of the mentally great as there is the general limitation of the mentally small. The men and women who should grapple with opportunity find their knees loosened beneath them in the struggle. The questing vision of the pioneer is made as nothing by the questing beast of sexual passion. Or else it is greed, jealousy, petty ambition that slip in to assassinate promise. The men who should be leaders of the New Republic become the slaves of desire. Consider the central subjects of three of these novels. Ponderevo's darting mind is apprenticed to the art and craft of legalised swindling; Remington's statesmanship founders on that rock where the career of Parnell was sunk; Trafford with his zest and talent for the arduous complexities of research finds the business of home life too much for him. It is easier to be a genius than a husband; it is easier to sketch a new Jerusalem than to implement a marriage of true minds; it is easier to build a thousand Utopian castles in the air than to move one's

THE HUMAN LIMITATION

own body but one inch from the slime of to-day. The human limitation does more than fetter the march of a nation; it trips the leaders and snares the great elect. The brain is mighty, but the flesh is weak. And the spirit bloweth where it listeth, and by no means at reason's behest. That is the tragedy, as it is also the comedy, of the human limitation.

The riddle for the statesman-philosopher, however, cannot be thus simply stated and left for the scrutiny of mankind. In that very poignant and very wise letter which Margaret wrote to Remington when he had broken with his career for the sake of Isabel and his illicit, surpassing passion the deserted wife thus touches on the human limitation:

"There's this difference that has always been between us, that you like nakedness and wildness, and I, clothing and restraint. You are always talking of order and system, and the splendid dream of the order that might replace the muddled system you hate, but by a sort of instinct you seem to want to break the law. I've watched you so closely. Now I want to obey laws, to make sacrifices, to follow rules. I don't want to make, but I do want to keep. You are at once makers and rebels, you and Isabel too. You're bad people—criminal people, I feel, and yet full of something the world must have. You're so much better than me, and so much viler."

"Yet full of something the world must have." That is the second aspect of the riddle. There is the inherent conflict and contradiction in social growth. Mere orderliness, may it not grow sterile? The law-making, law-abiding man, may he not lack within his solid substance the creative spark that may set the world on fire, to its ruin, and yet may also illumine it, to its great benefit and glory? There is no smoke without fire; there is no light without heat. And with heat there is destruction. There are strength and vast potential values in the human limitation.

Wells saw that clearly, and in these pre-war novels the balance is fairly held between

THE HUMAN LIMITATION

wildness and restraint. There is no solution of the statesman's riddle, but there are hints for a hundred solutions. There is no final philosophy of sex, but there are hints for a hundred readjustments of the social machinery into which this particular form of the human limitation goes dangerously bursting. It must be remembered that the Britain in which these pre-war novels were written, and of which they are brilliantly representative, was being torn and tortured by the suffrage conflict that now seems so distant and so curious. The one really big and durable change in the social scene of Britain made by the war has been in the status of women. The coming of the profiteers and the decay of the middle-class have been absurdly over-emphasised. All through history " the gentry " have been raging against " the nouveaux riches," and though the war helped the manufacturer to put a spurt on his social advance he was caught in the post-war slump. The public schools are still filled by the sons of the fathers who were there before them. The governing class has held its position after some initial surrenders and not a few labours in recapture. Those who hunted with the Quorn before hunt with the Quorn to-day. Horseback Hall has held its own despite much argument, mostly sentimental, to the contrary.

But the middle-class daughters have their latch-keys. The professions are open to the educated woman whose livelihood is no longer confined to the schoolroom. Women go where they please, and do as they please. "This freedom" for good or ill remains from the war. *The Wife of Sir Isaac Harman*, however much it may live as fiction, is dead as current social comment, quite as dead as the description of Bladesover in *Tono-Bungay*. Yet the more the sexes mingle in doing the world's work, the more surely will sexual infatuation and all the restlessness born of jealousy and desire complicate the workaday life of men and women. The sham-respectable Victorian home with its background of furtive masculine amours had a species of solidity about it. That has yielded to an equality

THE HUMAN LIMITATION

of the sexes which is an equality not only of votes, but of opportunity for vice and virtue. The war stretched out on its hard frame the narrow opinions about sexual restraint held by many good people. Post-war novelists create their " Ann Veronicas " by the score almost without comment.

Courageous people will welcome that liberation, even though it may intensify the perils of the human limitation in statecraft, and the guidance of all public affairs. The irruption had to come and its process is described by Wells in these novels with a vividness beyond praise. Mr Sidney Dark quotes in his book on *The Outline of H. G. Wells,* Wells' statement to Henry James: " I would rather be called a journalist than an artist." That fragment of self-description is capable of almost infinite discussion. What, for instance, is the difference in quality between a first-rate journalist and a first-rate artist ? One point, at any rate, can be firmly seized. The descriptive journalist is taking life's panorama in detail, working necessarily in haste and upon immediate impressions. As he writes, the panorama is altering. By the time his work has gone to press, the whole atmosphere may have altered, and the values of his emphasis be vitiated through no fault of his own. The strength of such work lies in its freshness and the kind of warmth and veracity that comes with immediate contact. Mr C. E. Montague, writing of dramatic criticism done for a daily paper with " hot air and dust of the playhouse still in the lungs," observes: "How bad it all was for measure, containment and balance! But that heat of the playhouse is not wholly harmful : . . . below yourself in certain ways, you hope you are above yourself in others." This is surely true of Wells' social criticism in the big pre-war novels. They lack the detached scrutiny of the artist who will ponder for a year before he puts pen to paper. Wells wrote, as the journalist writes, " with the hot air and dust of the playhouse " or Parliament house or salon still in the lungs. Below himself in some ways, he was above himself in others.

THE HUMAN LIMITATION

These studies in the victims of the human limitation are gusty, forcible, and sometimes violent, storming against the discipline of art. But they are instinct with life and quite unforgettable ; unforgettable as much in their very comedy as in their agonies and exaltations. Aunt Plessington and her breed linger in the mind with the Uncle Penstemons and the Chester Cootes. The reader should not go to them for grand or simple solutions. The problems of discipline and freedom, of character and circumstance, in which they deal, are beyond the settlement of verbal formulæ or rigid ideas. When at the end of *Marriage* Trafford and his wife seek to find the roots of the domestic issue in the wilds of Labrador, they can do no more than fruitfully suggest and explore veins of theory as miners explore veins of metal. " We want to understand," cries Trafford, " how people react upon one another to produce social consequences, and you ask me to put it at once in a draft bill for the reform of something or other." The early Wells had been a great drafter of

H. G. WELLS

ideal legislation; this Wells of the pre-war novels is chary of the draughtsman's desk. He is handling the pen of the writer with anger and with hope, and sometimes with a compassion for the blunders of mankind that sets the sails of beauty moving across the torrent of his words.

VI

FAITH AND MR BRITLING

WHEN the war came Wells took what one may call the average Liberal view. He was impatient of pacifism and of the critics of the Asquith-Grey policy. He wrote in the winter of 1914 a little book, *The War that Will End War*, putting in his own vigorous way the Liberal case against Germany. Germany was lawlessness; the Allies were for law. To the New Utopian, to the believer in the New Republic of order and control, there could be no choice but one. Germany's "might-politics" were the supreme expression of the old, disorderly, brawling world. Their suppression was the essential foundation of any sane and purposive social order.

During 1915 Wells published three books that are pre-war in temper and aspect. *Bealby* is a reversion to *Mr Polly's* type.

H. G. WELLS

Boon, published anonymously, is a collection of drawings and papers that contains a rather bitter parody of the too delicate literary method of Henry James and of his fictional creatures, that appear to have vastly more brain than blood. *The Research Magnificent* I have already grouped with the pre-war novels. Then in 1916 came *Mr Britling Sees It Through*. This ran in serial form in *The Nation*. When printed in book form it proved to be an enormous success, particularly with the reading public of the United States, who found that censored newspapers gave them a very meagre sense of the war's realities and of the intimate meaning of the struggle to those who were living in it or about its edge. Here at any rate were the war-view and war-philosophy of one of the ablest living Englishmen, a fresh and fearless testimony of the Liberal type of mind. First published in October, the book ran through edition after edition, and such success was not at all beyond its deserts.

Wells had always been a personal writer; never before had he been so personal as in

FAITH AND MR BRITLING

this document that covers fifteen months of war, as seen and felt in Matching's Easy, which represents Wells' Essex home at Little Easton, where he had settled after leaving his house in Church Row, Hampstead. Mr Sidney Dark identifies the characters in *Mr Britling*. " Colonel Rendezvous is the highly competent soldier who for some time commanded the Canadian Army in France and is now known as Lord Byng. The journalist is Ralph Blumenfeld, the American-born editor of *The Daily Express*; Lawrence Carmine is Cranmer Byng, the Oriental scholar and poet." And Mr Britling, of course, is self-portraiture, though the family history and the loss of the son Hugh are added for the story's purpose. This Mr Britling is not a novelist, but a publicist and leader-writer, a man of immensely fertile mind and fired with a generous passion for ideas. Mr Britling's story has no particular " plot," in the commonly accepted sense. His son enlists and is killed. His secretary enlists and is long described " wounded and missing "—luckily to return at last.

H. G. WELLS

Mr Britling is visited by an American intellectual, Mr Direck, who argues and criticises and puts the American point of view and finally enlists with the Canadians. And then, in the autumn of 1915, the record ends. How little there appears to be in that naked account! How much of wisdom and of feeling there is, in fact, in this profound and moving document!

I would add to the words " profound and moving " the further adjectives " sensitive " and " beautiful." The sourness that gave to the pre-war novels an occasional and rasping acidity has gone. There is no bitterness here, except against the perverse, obstinate, Kaiserish type of English Toryism that may be summed up as " Carsonism." For the spite and blustering of Ulster politics Wells has no mercy, but for the most part human fallibility, though not ignored, comes lightly off in this book, which has a mellowness of tone in harmony with its high quality of social speculation. Into the passage describing the announcement of Hugh's death there comes a masterful and beautiful

FAITH AND MR BRITLING

compassion that is unequalled in Wells' writing, save possibly in the closing chapters of *The New Machiavelli*, and particularly in Margaret's last letter to Remington. Mrs Britling, Hugh's stepmother, could not reach her husband with her sympathy; there was a temperamental estrangement.

"The door had hardly shut upon her before he forgot her. Instantly he was alone again, utterly alone. . . . Across the dark he went and suddenly his boy was all about him, playing, climbing the cedars, twisting miraculously about the lawn on a bicycle, discoursing gravely upon his future, lying on the grass, breathing very hard, and drawing preposterous caricatures. Once again they walked side by side up and down—it was athwart this very spot—talking gravely but rather shyly. . . .

"And here they had stood a little awkwardly before the boy went in to say good-bye to his stepmother and go off with his father to the station. . . .

"'I will work to-morrow again,' whispered Mr Britling, 'but to-night—to-night . . . To-night is yours. Can you

H. G. WELLS

hear me ? Can you hear ? Your father . . . who had counted on you . . .' "

It shall not be said that there is no tenderness in Wells' work. To countless parents across the world those moments came. Wells spoke for all : for the father of Herr Heinrich, the pleasant, docile, German tutor of the young Britlings, as for Mr Britling himself, whom loneliness struck like a blow.

The social criticism which is as much the essence of the book as the mental and spiritual progress of Mr Britling, is a riper, deeper thing than any previous brilliance of the Wellsian method. The book starts with Matching's Easy at peace, and from his Essex windows Britling-Wells gets a larger view of the English countryside than ever did young Ponderevo-Wells from Bladesover.

" He was inordinately proud of England and he abused her incessantly. He wanted to state England to Mr Direck as the amiable summation of a grotesque assembly of faults. That was the view into which the comforts and prosperities of his middle age had brought him from a radicalism that had in its earlier stages been angry and bitter."

Could England's rural life be better hit off in a single phrase than by this " amiable summation of a grotesque assembly of faults," a summation which left Mr Britling critical and happy, and certainly more proud than peevish ?

Over it all, green fields and urban squalor and London's grandeur, lay in that June of 1914 the conviction of utter, unassailable security, a sense of still life that has never come back to us since and never can return until both the international and industrial problems have been so wisely and so completely broken down by sanity, justice and tolerance that the words " war " and " class-war " remain as mere antiquities in our language. As Mr Britling put it :

" It's just because we are all convinced that we are so safe against a general breakdown that we are able to be so recklessly violent in our special cases. Why shouldn't women have the vote ? they argue. What does it matter ? And bang goes a bomb in Westminster Abbey. Why shouldnt Ulster create an impossible position ? And off trots some demented Carsonite to Germany to play at treason on some half word of the German Emperor's and buy half-a-million rifles. . . . Exactly like children being very, very naughty."

And then Sarajevo, the ultimata, the parleying, the war. At Matching's Easy, as in Paris, Berlin, Petrograd, and all the scenes of scurrying mobilisation and blind, tumultuous emotion,

"the familiar scenery of life was drawn aside, and War stood unveiled. 'I am the Fact,' said War, 'and I stand astride the path of life. I am the threat of death and extinction that has always walked beside life, since life began. There can be nothing else and nothing more in human life until you have reckoned with me.'"

Mr Britling began, as most men began, with the easy belief that a few months would see it through. More quickly than most men he allowed his eyes to be opened. The national instinct of treating any great occurrence as a joke and the idiotic propaganda of " business as usual " could only vex his sense and sting his sensibility. Then came his realisation of the fact of Malignity. Man could hate and in his hate he could lie and scream and deny all the elements of his manhood. " We are all fools still. Striving apes, irritated beyond measure by our own striving, easily moved to anger." And from that he passed on to Britain " in the web of the ineffective," given over as ever to short views and dread of orderly prevision,

" All along of dirtiness, all along of mess,
All along of doing things rather more or less."

The book contains some wonderful letters from Hugh Britling, first from his training quarters and then from the front. There are vivid criticisms of the blind eyes in the War Office and of the young British officer, as gallant as unintelligent, more ashamed of something wrong about his appearance than of muffing his job. There is an equally vivid statement of what war means to the combatant.

"War is an exciting game [wrote Hugh] that I never wanted to play. It excites one once in a couple of months. And the rest of it is dirt and muddle and boredom, and smashed houses and spoilt roads and muddy scenery and boredom, and the lumbering along of supplies and the lumbering back of the wounded and weary—and boredom, and continual vague guessing of how it will all end and boredom and boredom and boredom and thinking of all the work you were going to do and the travel you were going to have. . . ."

Then came the defeats, the disillusion, the gradual dawning on men's minds of the meaning of the struggle ahead and of the quality of our leaders. "What's the good of all this clamouring for a change of Government? We haven't a change of Government. It's like telling a tramp to get a change of linen. Our public men, all our public men, are second-rate men with

FAITH AND MR BRITLING

the habits of advocates. There is nothing masterful in their minds."

With the news of Hugh's death Mr Britling's mind rose above the eddies of the day, and he is left writing "an essay of preposterous ambitions" on "The Better Government of the World," and making a statement of first and last things to the parents of Herr Heinrich, who had also been killed in this "massacre of boys." And as he writes there comes to him what is almost a vision of God, certainly a sense of God, not as something infinite and omnipotent, but as a friend and helper, needing always our friendship and our help, not anthropomorphic, yet not coldly inhuman. This God takes for him the form of a King and Captain in a voluntary co-partnership of progress.

"He is the only King. Of course I must write about Him. I must tell all my world of Him. And before the coming of the true King, the inevitable King, the King who is present whenever just men foregather. This blood-stained rubbish of the ancient world, these puny kings and tawdry lawyers, these men who claim and grab and trick and compel, these war-makers and oppressors, will presently shrivel and pass, like paper thrust into a flame."

There Mr Britling ends. But Wells was aflame with the idea of God, and during the next year of his work it was to dominate his intention and mould his whole philosophy of the individual and the common life.

To understand the war-found religion of Wells we must, however, look back at his previous speculation. Wells was never a materialist and never interpreted religion as a gigantic fraud or blunder, for which the foxiness of priests and the innocence of laymen was responsible. He could not visualise the universe except as a unity and a system, and he did not object to calling such a vision of coherence and purpose a faith in God. His Samurai in *A Modern Utopia* accept a relationship between God and man with the qualification that "the aspect of God is different in the measure of every man's individuality." The God of the Samurai

FAITH AND MR BRITLING

is mystical and transcendental, to be found in silent communings in desert places. The Samurai go into the loneliness in quest of God as Trafford and his wife went at the end of *Marriage* to Labrador in quest of truth and a practical discipline for the better ordering of life,

In *First and Last Things* (1908) there is explicit affirmation of belief, but it will hardly satisfy an eager deist:

"I believe in the scheme, in the Project of all things, in the significance of myself and of all life, and that my defects and ugliness and failures, just as much as my powers and successes, are things that are necessary and important and contributory in that scheme, that scheme which passes my understanding—and that no thwarting of my conception, not even the cruelty of nature, now defeats or can defeat my faith, however much it perplexes my mind."

That faith implies a purpose, not a Person. In the same book Wells finds "the Christian theology Aristotelean, over-defined and excessively personified," and the Christ of whom he writes as the Christ we know is "a conception, a synthesis of emotions, experiences and inspirations, sustained by and sustaining millions of human souls." After this follows a criticism of the Christian Christ as being too sinless, too fine, lacking the human touch. To the man of petty weaknesses and the human limitation this unlimited virtue and excellence must seem cold and forbidding. Wells craves a more blundering, finite leader. And so it comes to this :

"I think Christianity has been true, and is for countless people practically true, but that it is not true now for me, and that for most people it is true only with modifications. Every believing Christian is, I am sure, my spiritual brother, but if systematically I called myself a Christian, I feel that to most men I should imply too much and so tell a lie."

As far as I can sum up the theology of Wells in 1908 it may be reduced to this. The world is the expression of a scheme; it is held together by some purpose, perplexing, but not insoluble. The personal twist

FAITH AND MR BRITLING

given to this purpose by religions, and particularly by Christianity, must be judged by the pragmatic test. Does it work, does it help? Christianity is true for those whom it helps. It must be valued by its results. That is as far as we can go.

But in two books published in 1917 Wells does go much further, taking up the religious issue where Mr Britling left it. *God, The Invisible King* is an essay in faith; *The Soul of a Bishop* is the same essay in fictional clothing. In Wells' new faith there are two Gods. One is the Creator, whom he calls the Veiled Being. This is the ultimate cause of things, a force remote and inscrutable. It may be called a phase of the Life Force. It is a God that a disbeliever in God might almost accept. But nearer to us is the God of the Human Heart, a finite, personal, struggling, apprehensible God. He is not transcendent, but immanent. He bears some relation to the God in Tennyson's *Higher Pantheism*, so bitterly parodied by Swinburne. He is about us, in us, on our side. One of the best Victorian defences of religion is to be found in " Bishop Blougram's Apology," but there is a curious difference between the God of Bishop Blougram and the God of Bishop Scrope, the central figure in *The Soul of a Bishop*:

" Just when we are safest, there's a sunset-touch,
A fancy from a flower-bell, some one's death,
A chorus-ending from Euripides,—
And that's enough for fifty hopes and fears
As old and new at once as Nature's self,
To rap and knock and enter in our soul,
Take hands and dance there, a fantastic ring,
Round the ancient idol, on his base again,—
The grand Perhaps ! "

" Safest " in the first line of course means safe in scepticism. This God of Blougram's comes in as an afterthought, by hints and fancy and suggestion. But Wells' God comes in a blaze. Either this Invisible King of man's purpose is known by the vision splendid, or he is not known at all. For Mr Britling suddenly " God was beside him, and within him, and about him." The mind of Bishop Scrope "was saturated as it had never been before by his sense of the immediate presence of God. He floated in that realisation. He was not so much thinking now as conversing starkly with the divine interlocutor, who penetrated all things and saw into and illuminated every recess of his mind."

"God, as Scrope saw in his third vision, was coming into the life of all mankind in the likeness of a captain and a king; all the governments of men, all the leagues of men, their debts and claims and possessions, must give way to the world republic under God the King. For five troubled years he had been staring religion in the face, and now he saw that it must mean this—or be no more than fetishism, Obi, Orphic mysteries or ceremonies of Demeter, a legacy of mental dirtiness, a residue of self-mutilation and superstitious sacrifices from the cunning, fear-haunted, ape-dog phase of human development."

This creed is a creed of God, not of Christ. It means an entire revaluation of Christian doctrine, and that restatement involves a repudiation of the Trinity and of all the mental ingenuities which were grafted on to the simple doctrine of the Kingdom of God by the pettifogging theorists of the early churches. The villain of the piece is Athanasius, portrayed as a little red-haired wirepuller, endeavouring to noose eternity in epigrams. Scrope, convinced of the new faith, abandons the old. The soul of the bishop is saved by the loss of the bishopric. He told his Confirmation candidates how narrow, fearful, suspicious and conservative men had sought in every age to imprison faith in formulæ and to embalm the living belief in documents as though it would otherwise become corrupt. So they have lost God. That, of course, was too much for Anglicanism. Scrope resigned to follow his King alone.

This Invisible King, mysteriously apprehended and not susceptible to closely reasoned approach, is our leader and our ally in the march towards an ordered world. He is our fellow-soldier against sect and

FAITH AND MR BRITLING

strife, and the festering acquisitive spirit of shoddy commercialism. He is, I think it is fair to say, a personation of the Utopian, a prototype of the good citizen who fights (there is no quietism or pacifism about this King) for his ideal of clean, courageous living.

There is no use in argument about the authenticity of religious experience. To one man this vivid, personal God will seem no more than a good friend, and therefore no God at all. To another he will seem unreal, intrusive; to another sentimental. To yet another the vision will come, not to be denied or forgotten or fobbed off. None of these men will be able to prove his point against the other any more than he can prove that two and two make four. There are ultimate things, matter for intuition not for logic. To a sceptic's temperament this notion of God is antipathetic, simply because he has not felt it, and he would ask why it is that the apprehension of God comes to so few. Millions are denied it, although they in no way fight against it.

H. G. WELLS

Why is this King so partial in the distribution of his presence? But that is no argument in the eyes of those who have had the vision, and to talk to them wisely about illusions or self-persuasion will not persuade them one jot to go back upon their faith which is born of a seeming miracle. Nor would there be any profit in asking them to explain, if they can, the problem of evil, or to state more explicitly the relation of the Heart-God to the Cause-God. Those who have felt have felt, and that is the end of it.

VII

THE HOPE THAT IS IN HISTORY

DURING the last year of the war Wells published *Joan and Peter*. It is a very long novel, in bulk, I should think, quite his largest story. It is partly a further record of Britain during the war, and partly a critical essay on modern education. As an interpretation of the national temper during that terrific national strain it is intermittently profound. Sometimes, as in his portrait of the pacifists, Wells is more waspish than illuminating; sometimes, as in the conversations of Oswald Sydenham, he reaches his familiar level of eloquent statesmanship. There is some biting satire of Lady Charlotte Sydenham, the old Tory lady with a hot belief in Ulster's loyalty and the detestable, invincible selfishness and cowardice of the British poor. Both the war-critical and

H. G. WELLS

educational-constructional sides of this book may be harmonised if we regard it as a discourse on the British mind, its inertia in peace, its failure in war and its possible salvation by knowledge and discipline in the world after the war.

Wells speaks through the mouth of Oswald:

" What has the history of education always been ? A series of little teaching chaps trying to follow up and fix the fluctuating boundaries of communities like an insufficient supply of upholsterers trying to overtake and tack down a carpet that was blowing away in front of a gale. . . . They were trying to do something they hadn't clearly defined. . . . This League of Free Nations, of which all men are dreaming and talking, this world republic, is the rediscovered outline, the proper teaching of all real education, the necessary outline now of human life. . . . This idea of a world-wide commonwealth, this ideal of an everlasting world-peace in which we are to live and move and have our being, has to be built up in every school, in every mind, in every lesson."

THE HOPE THAT IS IN HISTORY

Wells was not preaching at large, or merely in terms of pious aspiration. He determined to provide a text-book for this new conception of history as one story, and of history as our guide to a world made one, and so safe and spacious for the generations that shall follow. He set to work accordingly with tireless energy and burning faith in the value of his job to make this world-history with his own hands, not exulting in any superior wisdom of his own, but claiming that, if the historians would not do their obvious and proper work, he would have to do it for them as best he could.

Wells published *The Outline of History* in 1920. It carries the stamp of his personality all over it, and is accordingly the most vivid history-book in the English language as far as an ordinary reader's experience goes. It is probably the most vivid history-book in the world, if you discount the Old Testament on the ground of its being poetry and fiction as well as history. But the excitement comes from the subject, which is

H. G. WELLS

the adventure of man upon earth, as much as from the narrative skill of the historian. This is not the brilliant, gusty, discursive Wells of the novels, but Wells engaged on the most solemn and splendid work of his life, which is to supply the world with those common historical ideas "without which there can be no common peace or prosperity." Just as the nations can no longer live without some supernational control, so their separate, national, semi-partisan history-writing must be superseded by some document of man's doings and sufferings which shall be more than a mere aggregate of the partisan writings, in short, a supernational history. Wells did not content himself with preaching his doctrine of salvation through knowledge. He determined to see that the chance of knowledge abounded, to make that saving knowledge available by the toil of his own brain and hands. The immensity of that task is obvious from a mere glance at the *Outline*. Wells had helpers, of course, and very acute constructive criticism from such

THE HOPE THAT IS IN HISTORY

specialists as Sir E. Ray Lankester, Sir H. H. Johnston, Professor Gilbert Murray and Mr Ernest Barker. But no living Englishman save Wells could have made this book. Where else would be found such terrific energy, such fertility of mind, such an easy flow of luminous, descriptive prose?

I hold the *Outline* to be invaluable and I choose the epithet with purpose. At a guinea it is among the best bargains ever put before the serious reading public, and it is unique. There had been essays in " history as a whole " before, but never of this range and vision, never giving such quality of expression to such carefully garnered stores of information. Of course a few specialists may sneer at the irruption of the " generalist " into their preserves; of course some of the individual historical judgments are questioned and pooh-poohed. That was inevitable. The point is that for the average man who wants to discover both briefly and accurately how this world happened, how man lived, fought, thought, and grew from the emergence of the protoplasm to the Treaty of Versailles, this is an answer. Brief it is (and briefer still in *The Short History of the World* which Wells published in 1922) and wise it is. For it is more than a catalogue of the crimes and follies of mankind: it is a guide to the Salvaging of Civilisation and to a World Set Free.

The *Outline* should be the first of a series of documents for the General Training of the Citizen. Education in this country was, until 1870, a limited, particularised business for the wealthy class. It was an introduction to gentility by way of Greece and Rome. National education came as an introduction to office and workshop by way of the three R's. It was not and is not a training for manhood and womanhood. It is a smattering for barest trade purposes. Children are turned out of the schools when they have been taught to read, but not to think. For them cater the great Press lords, with their newspaper and magazine and novelette factories. That is the vision of life that awaits them. And what a vision! A great newspaper proprietor was once defined as

THE HOPE THAT IS IN HISTORY

the man who smashed the purpose of the Education Acts. Meanwhile the privileged public school and university student continues his introduction to gentility or to a professional career in an education which is specialised and sterile. It may store the memory, but it does not often kindle the fancy. It may often make the successful examinee, it rarely creates the informed, alert and critical citizen. A classical education is still a thing of rags and patches, and though the patches may be of finest quality and richest embroidery they are patches none the less. It goes on for twelve or thirteen years with magnificent expensiveness, and at the end its most gifted student may be, and probably will be, ludicrously ignorant of what happened to the world before 300 B.C. and after A.D. 100. I write bitterly, from my own experience.

General statements on such a subject are of little value compared with a summary of fact, and the writer accordingly must state his own adventures in education, not because he believes himself to be of the slightest

H. G. WELLS

interest as an individual, but because he knows himself to be one among many. He was put to Latin at seven, to Greek at ten ; that, no doubt, was the right thing, since he was doing other things as well. But from fifteen to twenty-two he had practically no teaching whatever outside the range of the classics. At fifteen he took the Higher Certificate, which meant that he need do no more mathematics, but took " Extra Classics " instead. At sixteen he was compelled to drop French and take " Extra Special Classics." He never had one minute's teaching in modern languages or science. English history shared its annual turn in a three-year cycle with Roman and Greek history ; thus in five years a boy might have four years' ancient to one year's modern history if he entered upon the cycle at a particular time. He had one hour a week of English literature and occasional English essays to write. Divinity meant Greek Testament. All else was the classics. At the public school in question there were no " out-of-school " interests encouraged except

THE HOPE THAT IS IN HISTORY

athletics. There was no teaching of the principles of architecture, no lectures by Labour leaders, or repertory dramatists or poets or painters of the day; there were no trips to local antiquities; geography after the fourth form meant ancient geography. And there was practically no leisure outside the routine of work and play in which a boy could explore new avenues for himself.

Yet this travesty of an education did the trick it was intended to do. It won a university scholarship. Then followed four more years in which the teaching was, with the exception of some modern philosophy, all purely classical. That again did the trick and obtained the required degrees. At the age of twenty-two the writer was in a position to look back upon eight years of complete specialisation, of total immersion in classical waters. He could not question the capacity of this training to do the requisite tricks; it guaranteed a gentleman's livelihood in some sort, either by teaching at school or university or by a post in the Civil Service. Yet he could not but feel humiliated

H. G. WELLS

in the presence of his own abysmal ignorance of the world. For the world as he knew it began about 500 B.C. and stopped short at A.D. 69. Within those narrow limits he had a short-lived treasury of detail, and he had, of course, enjoyed the freedom of rare intellects, of epics and tragedies and orations and philosophies that remain abidingly to tingle in the mind. He had enjoyed great privilege: Homer and Euripides, Lucretius and Catullus, Plato and Herodotus—all these and many others had been handed to him for most intimate acquaintance. Yet, with the exception of modern philosophy, there was nothing else that had come except by breaking bounds on his own initiative and at the cost of falling behind with his classics. No science, no modern languages save schoolboy French, no English literature, no geography, no modern history, no training in handicraft had come into the curriculum. Shades of the prison-house indeed! And though his places of confinement had been Hellenic temple and Roman Capitol, filled with a nipping and an eager air, they were

THE HOPE THAT IS IN HISTORY

none the less a prison. It is no light business for a man to start to educate himself at twenty-two or three, when the mind has been moulded and the memory stiffened. Is there nothing here for blame, nothing for anger ?

What has all this to do with the *Outline* ? It is simply one of the many justifications for such a book and for similar books that will clarify and co-ordinate the world for people whose education has either been trivial or intensely and narrowly specialised. The *Outline* is a hint of all the effectual antidotes that have yet to be found for the education of squalid rags or brilliant patches. It is simple enough to be understood by those whose schooling was cut short in childhood ; it is advanced enough for those who carry university distinctions. It is also a highly potent vaccine to be used against the infection of the merely nationalist, sectional and propagandist history that it suits lazy-minded or unscrupulous people to keep fermenting in the schools.

The *Outline* was hotly criticised. Inevitably it gave offence to Roman Catholics. Classicists were horrified by Wells' attitude to Greece and Rome. Hero-worshippers found such conventional heroes as Cæsar and Alexander, Napoleon and Mr Gladstone appearing as peculiarly small and faded figures in the hard, clear light of the centuries. Wells wanted criticism. Some he answered by pamphlet, some he accepted, and one or two of his sweeping judgments were removed by the time of the 1923 edition. The *Outline* is to be a continuous, organic book. It will be constantly kept up to date, refreshed, revised. New additions to old knowledge will be grafted on to it. It will be continued, as it began, as " an attempt to tell how our present state of affairs, this distressed and multifarious human life about us, arose in the course of vast ages and out of the inanimate clash of matter and to estimate the quality and amount and range of the hopes with which it now faces its destiny."

One day in July I met in Oxford an examiner who had been coping with hundreds

THE HOPE THAT IS IN HISTORY

of history papers done by boys and girls competing for Higher Certificates. He moaned over the answers given, not because they were wrong in fact or careless in expression, but because they were so utterly machine-made. "There's not one in five hundred," he said, "who seems to be really excited by the world or to have any sense of wonder." A sense of wonder is exactly what the *Outline* creates. Challenge its details and its personal judgments as you may, you cannot deny that it stirs the mind irresistibly. It has provoked some angry retorts; I doubt whether it has ever induced boredom.

VIII

SINCE THE WAR

WELLS' work since the war has been mainly by way of restatement and re-emphasis and adjustment of his views on world politics to the world situation. There has been no distinct and different phase of his writing. In 1919 he published *The Undying Fire,* which he calls " A Contemporary Novel," but which is better described as a debate on eternal mysteries. It is the Book of Job brought up to date. Job Huss, a reforming schoolmaster, whose evangel is the education of Wells' ideal, falls into dire misfortune; his school is burned, his money is lost, his position is threatened by dismissal, his life by cancer. The essence of the book is a long discussion held during the hours before a surgical operation. Job puts the case for despair in the face of a dreadful world.

SINCE THE WAR

"There is no reason anywhere, there is no creation anywhere, except the undying fire, the spirit of God in the hearts of men . . . which may fail . . . which may fail . . . which seems to me to fail." The book ends with a betterment of Job's fortunes. The story, however, does not much matter. The story has never been very real. The debate over the combat of good and evil forces in the world is realistic philosophy and has the authentic excitement of great conflict.

In 1920 Wells published the *Outline*, which we have already discussed, and *Russia in the Shadow*, the result of a personal investigation of the Bolshevik rule. Wells was attracted by the "realism" of the Russians displayed in their resolute pursuit of discipline; the Bolsheviks found a country in anarchic ruin and employed brutally stern methods to fashion an order of their own liking. Their policy had the merits of zeal, the limitations of a pedantic Marxian cult. Since Wells' visit the Marxian idolatry has notably ebbed away.

In 1921 came a volume on *The Salvaging*

of Civilisation. It is an essay on "The World State" as opposed to a World of Leagued Nations. There is bitter criticism of the League as constituted, which may be worse than nothing rather than better than nothing. "For this League of Nations at Geneva, this little corner of Balfourian jobs and gentility, no man would dream of fighting, but for the great state of mankind men will presently be very ready to fight." The world has a long way to go before it is ready to sink its nationalist preconceptions, and the statement that "the ploughing has been done, and the seed is in the ground, and the world state stirs in a multitude of germinating minds" strikes one in 1923 as too loosely optimistic. This book has a particularly interesting chapter on the formation of public opinion by "College, Newspaper and Book." In 1921 Wells also published in a pamphlet on *The New Teaching of History* his answer to some criticism of the *Outline.*

In the winter of 1921 Wells attended the Washington Conference on Disarmament. He went as the representative of *The*

SINCE THE WAR

Daily Mail, and his articles were widely "syndicated" across the world. His attitude to the obstructive nationalism of the French delegates proved too much for the tolerance of *The Daily Mail,* who printed no more of his messages after his attacks on France, "with her submarines and Senegalese." Subsequent messages of his were printed in England by *The Daily Express* and *The Manchester Guardian.* The articles were published in 1922 under the title of *Washington and the Hope of Peace.* A sentence may sum up the gist of the book, which contains a general approval of President Harding's notion of an Association of Nations.

"I have written of the defects of the League of Nations scheme, its premature explicitness, its thinly theoretical and imitative forms, its frequent mere camouflage, as in the mandatory system, of existing wrongs, and I have brought into contrast with it this newer and I think more natural and hopeful project of successive Conferences, throwing off Committees, embodying their results in treaties and Standing Commissions, and growing at last not so much into a World Parliament, which I perceive more and more clearly is an improbable dream, as into a living, growing organic network of World Government."

In the same year there was another novel, *The Secret Places of the Heart*, which begins like *The Soul of a Bishop* and *The Undying Fire* with a visit to the doctor. Sir Richmond Hardy, who is busily engaged upon the work of a National Fuel Commission, suffers from what is commonly known as " a nervous breakdown " and goes westward on a motor-tour with a doctor who wants him to ease his mind as well as his body. There is much good debate about the world at large and, incidentally, a wonderful description and imaginative reconstruction of the Wiltshire downs where British history began. Visitors to Avebury and Silbury and Stonehenge should put this book in their knapsacks ; it is worth a myriad " guides."

Up to the time of writing (September, 1923) Wells had published only one book in

SINCE THE WAR

1923—namely, *Men Like Gods*, a Utopian romance, in which Mr Barnstaple, a junior editor of *The Liberal*, finds himself along with some thinly disguised modern people of notability or notoriety whirled into futurity. This " Utopia has no parliament, no politics, no private wealth, no business competition, no police, no prisons, no lunatics, no defectives nor cripples, and it has none of these things because it has schools and teachers who are all that schools and teachers can be. Politics, trade and competition are the methods of adjustment of a crude society. Our education is our government." The book may be summarised as a post-war Wellsian variation on a pre-war Wellsian method.

There we must leave Wells, with great achievement behind him and great achievement to come. A newspaper which not long ago published a cartoon of Wells gave to it the title " The Weary Titan of the Western World." The weariness was certainly suggested by the sadness of the eyes, a sadness on which the cartoonists seize at some

H. G. WELLS

violence to the real truth. Mr Britling, it may be remembered, was continually " missed " in portraiture. I entirely fail to see how Wells can be described as a " weary " man ; when it comes to cleaning up the undergrowth of human prejudice and muddle he has the devastating energy of a forest-fire. The speed of his work is tremendous and, when one considers the amount of reading as well as the amount of writing that went to make the *Outline*, the application of the man is seen to be as far above the normal as is his imaginative fertility. St John Ervine in *Some Impressions of My Elders* reveals very graphically the restless activity of Wells, who is a great player of games, and yet is often slipping imperceptibly out of the game to work at a manuscript in his study. As he roughs out some new kingdom for man's spirit his mind darts into the unknown with the terrifying speed of a race-horse, and the writing hand must be very quick indeed to keep up with so fleet a mind. In his angry moods Wells seems to go exploding destructively and

SINCE THE WAR

untiringly amongst the follies and foibles of the day, like one of the atomic bombs of which he as written; indeed, among the literary leaders of our day he is definitely the most radio-active, a spinning atom of suggestion warmed by satiric fire. " You can almost lie in bed and hear him grow," was Mr Chesterton's way of visualising Wells the unweary. A shrewd observer of history remarked the other day that Europe is suffering from a deluge of radio-active politicians. To check their disastrous lack of vision and furious partisan temper the radio-active mind of Wells works without remission and with a temper too of its own. Critics of Wells sometimes find themselves placed like those who have been too close to the tiger's gaze — there is a flashing claw and the dust rises. Wells displays a brilliance in controversy that can sear while it illumines. But brilliance it is, and the fire is undying.

A BIBLIOGRAPHY OF H. G. WELLS' PRINCIPAL WRITINGS

Select Conversations with an Uncle (*Lane*). 1895.
The Time Machine—An Invention (*Heinemann*). 1895.
*The Stolen Bacillus and Other Stories (*Macmillan*). 1895.
The Wonderful Visit (*Dent*). 1895.
The Island of Dr Moreau (*Heinemann*). 1896.
The Wheels of Chance (*Dent*). 1896
*The Plattner Story (*Macmillan*). 1897.
The Invisible Man (*Macmillan*). 1897.
The War of the Worlds (*Heinemann*). 1898.
When the Sleeper Wakes (*Nelson*). 1899. (Afterwards published (1911) in a revised and altered edition as *The Sleeper Awakes*.)
*Tales of Space and Time (*Macmillan*). 1899.
Love and Mr Lewisham (*Macmillan*). 1900.
Certain Personal Matters (*Unwin*). 1901.
Anticipations (*Chapman & Hall*). 1901.
The First Men in the Moon (*Macmillan*). 1901.
The Discovery of the Future. (A lecture given at the Royal Institute, 1902.)
The Sea Lady—A Tissue of Moonshine. 1902.
Mankind in the Making (*Chapman & Hall*). 1903.
The Food of the Gods (*Macmillan*). 1904.

* Volumes of short stories.

BIBLIOGRAPHY

A Modern Utopia (*Nelson*). 1905.
Kipps. The Story of a Simple Soul (*Macmillan*). 1905.
In the Days of the Comet (*Macmillan*). 1906.
The Future in America (*Chapman & Hall*). 1906.
First and Last Things (*Constable*). 1907.
The Misery of Boots (*Fabian Tract*). 1907.
Socialism and Marriage (*Fabian Tract*). 1908
New Worlds for Old (*Constable*). 1908.
The War in the Air (*Bell*). 1908.
Tono-Bungay (*Macmillan*). 1909.
Ann Veronica (*Unwin*). 1909.
The History of Mr Polly (*Nelson*). 1910.
The New Machiavelli (*Lane*). 1910.
The Country of the Blind (*Nelson*). 1911.
Floor Games (*Palmer*). 1911. (A book about play for children.)
Socialism and the Great State (*Harper*). 1911. (The book is by fifteen authors. Wells contributes the first and longest essay.)
Marriage (*Macmillan*). 1912.
The Passionate Friends (*Macmillan*). 1913.
Little Wars (*Palmer*). 1913. (A book about play for children.)
An Englishman Looks at the World (*Cassell*). 1914.
The World Set Free (*Macmillan*). 1914.
The Wife of Sir Isaac Harman (*Macmillan*). 1914.
The War that will End War (*Palmer*). 1914.
The Research Magnificent (*Macmillan*). 1915.
Boon (under the pseudonym of " Reginald Bliss ") (*Unwin*). 1915.

H. G. WELLS

Bealby, a Holiday (*Methuen*). 1915.
Mr Britling Sees It Through (*Cassell*). 1916.
What is Coming ? (*Cassell*). 1916.
God the Invisible King (*Cassell*). 1917.
The Soul of a Bishop (*Cassell*). 1917.
In the Fourth Year (*Cassell*). 1918.
Joan and Peter (*Cassell*). 1918.
The Undying Fire (*Cassell*). 1919.
The Outline of History (*Cassell*). 1920.
Russia in the Shadow (*Hodder & Stoughton*). 1920.
The New Teaching of History (*Cassell*). 1921. (A reply to criticisms of the *Outline*.)
The Salvaging of Civilisation (*Cassell*). 1921.
The Secret Places of the Heart (*Cassell*). 1922.
A Short History of the World (*Cassell*). 1922.
Washington and the Hope of Peace (*Collins*). 1922.
Men Like Gods (*Cassell*). 1923.

AMERICAN BIBLIOGRAPHY

The Time Machine (*Holt*). 1895.
Select Conversations with an Uncle (*Merriam*). 1895.
The Wonderful Visit (*Macmillan*). 1895.
The Island of Doctor Moreau (*Stone & Kimball*). 1896.
The Wheels of Chance (*Macmillan*). 1896.
Thirty Strange Stories (*Edward Arnold*). 1897. (Transferred to *Harper*, 1898.)
The Invisible Man (*Edward Arnold*). 1897. (Transferred to *Harper*, 1898.)
The War of the Worlds (*Harper*). 1898.
When the Sleeper Wakes (*Harper*). 1899.
Tales of Space and Time (*Doubleday*). 1899.
Love and Mr Lewisham (*Stokes*). 1900.
Anticipations (*Harper*). 1901.
The First Men in the Moon (*Bobbs-Merrill Co.*). 1901.
The Discovery of the Future (*Smithsonian Institution*). 1902.
The Sea Lady (*Appleton*). 1902.
Mankind in the Making (*Scribner*). 1904.
The Food of the Gods (*Scribner*). 1904.
Twelve Stories and a Dream (*Scribner*). 1905.
A Modern Utopia (*Scribner*). 1905.
Kipps (*Scribner*). 1905.
In the Days of the Comet (*Century Co.*). 1906.
The Future in America (*Harper*). 1906.

H. G. WELLS

New Worlds for Old (*Macmillan*). 1908.
The War in the Air (*Macmillan*). 1908.
First and Last Things (*Putnam*). 1908.
Socialism and the Family (*Ball Publishing Co.*). 1908.
This Misery of Boots (*Ball Publishing Co.*). 1908.
Tono-Bungay (*Duffield*). 1909.
Ann Veronica (*Harper*). 1909.
The History of Mr Polly (*Duffield*). 1910.
The New Machiavelli (*Duffield*). 1910.
New York (*Brentano*). 1910. (An essay for a book of photogravure studies by Alvin Langdon Coburn.)
The Door in the Wall, and other Stories (*Kennerley*). 1911.
Socialism and The Great State (*Harper*). 1912. (A volume of essays, edited by H. G. Wells.)
Marriage (*Duffield*). 1912.
Floor Games (*Small*). 1912.
Little Wars (*Small*). 1913.
The Passionate Friends (*Harper*). 1913.
Social Forces in England and America (*Harper*). 1914.
The World Set Free (*Dutton*). 1914.
The Wife of Sir Isaac Harman (*Macmillan*). 1914.
The War that will End War (*Duffield*). 1914.
The End of the Armament Rings (Pamphlet) (*World Peace Foundation*). 1914.
Bealby (*Macmillan*). 1915.
Boon (*Doran*). 1915.
The Research Magnificent (*Macmillan*). 1915.

AMERICAN BIBLIOGRAPHY

What is Coming ? (*Macmillan*). 1916.
Mr Britling Sees It Through (*Macmillan*). 1916.
Italy, France and Britain at War (*Macmillan*). 1917.
God, the Invisible King (*Macmillan*). 1917.
The Soul of a Bishop (*Macmillan*). 1917.
In the Fourth Year (*Macmillan*). 1918.
Joan and Peter (*Macmillan*). 1918.
The Undying Fire (*Macmillan*). 1919.
The Outline of History (*Macmillan*). 1920. 2 vols.
Russia in the Shadows (*Doran*). 1921.
The Salvaging of Civilisation (*Macmillan*). 1921.
Washington and the Riddle of Peace (*Macmillan*). 1922.
The Secret Places of the Heart (*Macmillan*). 1922.
A Short History of the World (*Macmillan*). 1922.
Men Like Gods (*Macmillan*). 1923.

INDEX

ALEXANDER, 110
Ann Veronica, 63
Anticipations, 50, 51
Athanasius, 96

BARKER, Ernest, 103
Barnstaple, Mr, 117
Bealby, 38, 79
Belloc, Hilaire, 44, 56
Bennett, Arnold, 15, 18
Beresford, J. D., 33
Bladesover, 18, 63
Blougram, Bishop, 94
Bolsheviks, 113
Boon, 80
Bradlaugh, Charles, 13
Britling Sees It Through, Mr, 5, 46, 80 *et seq.*, 118
Bromley, 11
Bromstead, 15-17, 19

CÆSAR, Julius, 110
Carsonism, 82, 86, 99
Chaffery, 44
Chaplin, Charlie, 35
Chesterton, G. K., 43, 44, 54, 119
Chitterlow, 44
Christianity, 91 *et seq.*
Coote, Chester, 77
Cross, Victoria, 23

DARK, Sidney, 75, 81
Democracy, 75, 81
Dickens, Charles, 9, 43, 44
Direck, Mr, 82

EDUCATION, 100 *et seq.*
Einstein, 26
Eloi, 27
Ervine, St John, 118

FABIANS, 42, 55, 60
First and Last Things, 20, 58, 91
Food of the Gods, The, 33

GALSWORTHY, John, 15, 18
Garnett, Richard, 23
Gladstone, W. E., 13, 110
God the Invisible King, 93 *et seq.*
Great State, The, 56

HENLEY, W. E., 14, 23, 24
Herbert, Auberon, 13
Home Rule, 22
Hoopdriver, 39, 41
Hudson, W. H., 30
Huss, Job, 112, 113
Huxley, T. H., 13, 26

Island of Dr Moreau, The, 28, 29

JAMES, Henry, 75, 80
Joan and Peter, 99
John, Augustus, 62
Johnston, Sir H. H., 103

KAPEK, Dr, 29
Kensington, South, 13
Kipling, 23
Kipps, 38 *et seq.*

INDEX

Labrador, 77
Lane, John, 23
Lanketers, Sir E. Ray, 103
League of Nations, the, 100, 114, 115
Lenin, 53
Love and Mr Lewisham, 8

Mankind in the Making, 50
Marriage, 64, 77, 90
Matching's Easy, 81, 84
Men Like Gods, 117
Misery of Boots, This, 55
Modern Utopia, A., 50, 90
Montague, C. E., 76
Morlocks, 27
Morris, William, 13, 30
Murray, Prof. Gilbert, 103
Mussolini, Benito, 53

Napoleon, 110
National Schools, 17
New Machiavelli, The, 15, 64, 66
"New Republic," the, 52-54
New Teaching of History, The, 144
New Worlds for Old, 55

Orpen, Sir W., 62
Outline of History, The, 101 et seq., 118

Pall Mall Gazette, 21
Parnell, C. S., 70
Passionate Friends, The, 64
Penstemon, Uncle, 45
Plato, 54, 57, 58
Plessington, Aunt, 77
Polly, Mr, 17, 33, 38 *et seq*, 58, 79
Ponderevo, 70

Remington, 70, 71, 83
Research Magnificent, The, 20, 65
Robots, 29
Russia in the Shadow, 113

St John's Wood, 13
Salvaging of Civilisation, The, 20, 114
Samurai, 54, 55, 57, 90
Scott, Dixon, 55
Scrope, Bishop, 94
Secret Places of the Heart, The, 116
Select Conversations with an Uncle, 24, 26
Servile State, 56
Shakespeare, 9, 10, 66
Shaw, G. Bernard, 23, 61
Short History of the World, A, 104
Sleeper Awakes, The, 29
Smallways, Bert, 34
Socialism, 47 *et seq.*
Socialism and Marriage, 55
Soul of a Bishop, The, 94 *et seq.*, 116
Southsea, 13
Stolen Bacillus, the, 24
Sunderbund, Lady, 63
Sydenham, Oswald, 100

Tennyson, Alfred, Lord, 48, 93
Time-Machine, The, 13, 14, 24, 26
Tono-Bungay, 12, 46, 63
Trafford, 70, 77, 90
Turner, J. M. W., 10

Undying Fire, The, 112, 116

WALLAS, Graham, 48
War in the Air, The, 32, 34, 43
War of the Worlds, The, 32
War that Will End War, The, 79
Washington and the Hope of Peace, 115
Weller, Sam, 55
Wells, H. G., *passim*
Wells, Joseph, 11, 12

Wessex Novels, 23
Wheels of Chance, The, 38
Whitman, Walt, 19
Wife of Sir Isaac Harman, The, 64, 74
Wilson, Woodrow, 10
Wonderful Visit, The, 25
World Set Free, The, 32

Yellow Book, the, 23